Svend Otto S

Children of the Yangtze River

Translated by Joan Tate

PELHAM BOOKS

First published in Great Britain by Pelham Books Ltd,
44 Bedford Square, London WC1B 3DP in 1982

Reprinted 1985

First published in Denmark by Gyldendalske Boghandel
as *Børnene ved Yangtze Kiang* in 1982

Copyright © 1982 Svend Otto S
English translation Copyright © 1982 Pelham Books Ltd

All rights reserved. No part of this publication
may be reproduced, stored in a retrieval system, or
transmitted, in any form or by any means, electronic
mechanical, photocopying, recording or otherwise,
without the prior permission of the Copyright owner.

ISBN 0 7207 1432 X   Printed in Denmark

Right through the whole of China winds the Yangtze river.
In a house on the river bank lived Mei Mei. Chang lived in the house just above.

Mei Mei was on her way to school.

"Hurry up," she said to Chang. But first he had to shut his pig in, or it would follow him to school.

Chang's father was ploughing the rice fields, his water buffalo slowly pulling the plough through the mud.

"Hurry now!" shouted Chang's mother. "The bell's ringing."

"Look!" said Mei Mei. "I've got money for peanuts today."
Old Sung sold spices and beans and all kinds of things. Carefully, he poured nuts into her pocket without spilling a single one.

The bell was still ringing as they climbed up the hill. Everyone in the village could hear it.

In school, the first lesson was writing. There was a lot to learn, because there are thousands and thousands of picture-

words in Chinese, not just an alphabet.
This is what Mei Mei wrote:

$$我叫妹妹，我住在长江边上。$$

That means: My name is Mei Mei and I live by the Yangtze river.
Then the bell rang and the children all rushed out into the yard for gymnastics.

It was dinner time, so Chang and Mei Mei went home. On the way, they passed people sitting eating their rice under the awnings. At the tractor factory where Mei Mei's father worked, the men were sitting outside with their rice bowls.

"How's your pig?" they asked Chang. "Do you still keep it on a string?"

When they got back to Chang's house, his little brother and the little pig both squealed when they saw him.

Mei Mei went down to feed her birds. The birds sang all day as they hung there in their cages in the shade.

That evening, Mei Mei was lying in the big bed under the mosquito net. She was just about to fall asleep when she heard them talking about the river.

"It'll never get this far," said Grandfather. "I've lived here all my life and that's never happened before."

"But the radio said the rain in the mountains will make the river rise."

Then Mei Mei fell asleep.

The next morning, it was raining. Mei Mei was in such a hurry to tell Chang what she'd heard, she had no time to eat her morning rice.

"Have you heard? The river's rising and Father says it might come all the way up to us!" she said. Chang hadn't heard anything, but then his parents came in, looking worried.

"We must keep the animals in today," said Chang's father. "Until we've more news of the river."

But already the river was so high and the current so fast, the ferrymen had to row very hard just to get across the river.

They had only been in school an hour when they heard on the radio that the flood would reach its highest within twenty-four hours. Everyone living on the river bank would have to leave. The children were let out of school to go home and help.

"So it's true after all!" said Mei Mei, as they hurried down the steps.

At Chang's house, the clothes had already been packed up, as well as the precious rice, and the animals had been tied up. Chang tied his little pig's legs so that it couldn't run away.

All day, they heard about flooded villages further up the river and soldiers rescuing people and animals.

By the evening, the water was rising even faster. From Mei Mei's house, they could see the river was closer than ever.

The next morning, people started coming up the slope with their belongings. The old people who couldn't walk were being carried.

The people from the tractor factory were already going down to help.

The river was rushing and raging along, the water tumbling and tearing everything with it. Houses and trees floated down the river

and a pig was swirling round and round on a barn door. Three people clung to the roof of a house, shouting for help from the boatmen.

As the river heaved up and down, the boatmen pulled them into their boat.

Then it was the pig's turn to be rescued.
Everyone was leaving now as the river took one house after another.

The water had already reached Mei Mei's house as she took down her birds. Only the ducks and little Yang liked splashing in the water.

"Are you going to stay?" said Mei Mei, when she got to Chang's.

"Father hopes the water won't rise any more," said Chang. "But we're ready to go if we have to."

The animals had now all been collected together and tied up. Indoors, the water was all over the floor.

"I've never seen the water so high in all my life," said Grandfather. "Is the whole world about to go under?"

"We've got to go now," said Chang's mother to the old people. "They've come to help us."

One of the men carried Grandmother.
"I'll bet it's a long time since you last had a piggyback," he said cheerfully.

In the village, they were making huts of bamboo mats so that each family could have a room.

Now all the houses and fields had disappeared. Only the tops of the tallest trees showed above the water.

All the crops had been washed away. But the current was not so strong now and the wreckage floated more slowly down the muddy river.

The first night, they slept on the floor of the school. Chang hid his pig under his blanket.

Mei Mei hung her birds up under the roof and covered them up. But *she* couldn't sleep. Would they ever live in their house again?

The next day, everyone started fencing in the animals.

A week later, when the river had gone down and the sun had begun to dry out the fields, Chang and Mei Mei went down to see what their homes looked like.

Everything was changed. The green fields were covered with brown silt and mud from the river, and only Chang's house was left.

They started clearing up Chang's house. The water had come right inside and left mud everywhere, but Chang helped scoop it out with his bucket.

It was much worse at Mei Mei's. They found a few pots and pans, but the roof and walls had fallen down and there were deep cracks in the ground. Everywhere was the same.

The next day, Mei Mei ran over to Chang to tell him the exciting news.

"We're going to have a *new* house!" she cried. "We're *all* going to have new houses. But not by the river any more. They're going to build a whole new village for us further up."

Then the lorries came in a cloud of dust with stones and timber.

Down on the river, boat after boat arrived with heavy sacks of cement. Everyone helped to carry them up the slopes to where they were building the new village.

The children started planting the land as it was dug and cleared.

The silt the river had brought with it was very fertile and soon everything was growing in the hot sun.

When the houses were ready, everyone helped with the move. Mei Mei hung up her birds and the red good-luck sign by the door, and then the grandparents arrived.

The whole village had a party that day. They had firecrackers and fireworks, and there were lanterns in the trees.

It was a marvellous feast – fish from the river, roots of the lotus flower, swallow's nests and small crystallized apples, and finally a cake called "Dragon's Beard".

"Were you frightened when the river flooded, Mei Mei," said Chang's mother after the meal.

"A bit," said Mei Mei. "But when it really started, we had so much to do, we had no time to think."

"That's right," said her father. "No time to be afraid."